Robert E. Lee

Lee

Young Confederate

Illustrated by James Arthur
and
Gray Morrow

Robert E. Lee

Young Confederate

By Helen Albee Monsell

THE BOBBS-MERRILL COMPANY, INC.
INDIANAPOLIS/NEW YORK

PUBLISHED BY THE BOBBS-MERRILL CO., INC.
INDIANAPOLIS/NEW YORK

MANUFACTURED IN THE UNITED STATES OF AMERICA

Library of Congress Cataloging in Publication Data
Monsell, Helen Albee, 1895–
  Robert E. Lee, young Confederate.

  (Childhood of famous Americans)
  Reprint. Originally published: Boy of old Virginia,
Robert E. Lee. Indianapolis : Bobbs-Merrill, [c1937]
  Summary: A biography focusing on the childhood of the
man who turned down the field command of the United States
Army and became the leader of the Confederate Army during
the Civil War.
  1. Lee, Robert E. (Robert Edward), 1807–1870—Juvenile
literature.   2. Generals—United States—Biography—Juvenile
literature.   3. Confederate States of America. Army—Biography—Juvenile literature.
  [1. Lee, Robert E. (Robert Edward), 1807–1870.   2. Gen-
erals] I. Arthur, James, ill. II. Morrow, Gray, ill. III. Title.
IV. Series.
E467.1.L4M66   1983   973.7'092'4 [B] [92]   82-17848
ISBN 0–672–52750–2

To Mary Belle Johnston,
staunch daughter of the U.D.C.

Illustrations

Full pages

Numerous smaller illustrations

Contents

Books by Helen Albee Monsell

DOLLY MADISON: QUAKER GIRL
HENRY CLAY: YOUNG KENTUCKY ORATOR
JOHN MARSHALL: BOY OF YOUNG AMERICA
ROBERT E. LEE: YOUNG CONFEDERATE
SUSAN ANTHONY: GIRL WHO DARED
TOM JACKSON: YOUNG STONEWALL
TOM JEFFERSON: BOY OF COLONIAL DAYS
WOODROW WILSON: BOY PRESIDENT

★ Robert E. Lee

Lee

Young Confederate

Good-by to Stratford

WHEN ROBERT E. LEE was very small, he lived in a large house, called Stratford. There were woods and fields all around the house. Not far away was the Potomac River. It shone blue in the sunlight. The Lee family home was one of the prettiest places in all Virginia.

Something special was happening at Stratford on a fine summer morning in 1810. Robert was only three-and-a-half years old. He couldn't understand what was going on. He only knew that everything was a-hustle and a-bustle.

Wherever he went in the big house, someone was putting things in boxes or trunks.

11

In one of the bedrooms he found Mother and Mammy, the Negro nurse. Both of them were working busily. Mammy was bringing armsful of clothes to Mother. She was folding them carefully and putting them into a big trunk.

Robert ran to the trunk and looked in. He saw some of his own clothes. "Why are you putting my clothes in there?" he asked.

"We are packing them," Mother answered, but he knew from her tone of voice that she was only half-thinking about his question.

"Look, Mother!" Robert stood on tiptoe and pulled out a coat. "Here's a coat I haven't worn for a long time."

"Please, Robert," said Mother, "don't take things out of the trunk."

She took the coat and put it back in the trunk. "I wonder where the other children are," she said to Mammy. "I wish one of them would keep this little boy busy."

"Playing outside, probably," said Mammy.

Mother nodded. "Yes, they are old enough to realize they won't have such a fine place to play much longer."

Robert wondered what Mother meant. "Why won't they?" he asked.

Before anyone could answer, Smith came in. He was Robert's eight-year-old brother.

"Oh, there you are!" said Mother. "Why don't you and Robert go outside to play for a while?"

"I'm going around to say good-by to everybody on the plantation," said Smith. "Do you want to go with me, Robert?"

Of course Robert wanted to go. Perhaps Smith would tell him what was happening.

The two boys hurried from the room. As they went through the house, they saw Father sitting at his desk. He was sorting out letters and papers. Some of them he was tying into packages. Others he was throwing away.

Father's name was Henry Lee. He had been a hero in the Revolutionary War. His soldiers had given him the nickname of "Light-Horse Harry." The war had ended some years ago, but people still called Father Light-Horse Harry.

Robert was very proud of his father. He liked to be called Light-Horse Harry's son.

Now Robert stopped at the open door. Whatever Father was doing looked interesting. "Maybe," thought Robert, "if I go in and ask, he'll let me help tie up things. And maybe he'll tell me what is happening."

It was worth trying. Robert started through the door. "Father!" he called.

Father was so busy he didn't even look up.

Robert stopped. "Maybe," he decided, "I'd better go along with Smith."

By this time Smith was far ahead. He stopped, though, and waited for his little brother. "Let's go to the kitchen first," he said.

14

The kitchen was a small building. It was separate from the big house. The boys liked to go there because Aunt Cindy, the cook, made wonderful things to eat.

"We came to say good-by," Smith told her as he and Robert went into the kitchen.

Aunt Cindy was taking a pie from the oven.

"Um-um," said Smith. "That looks mighty good. Is it for us to eat on the road tomorrow?"

The old woman nodded her head.

"It smells mighty good, too," said Robert. "I'd like a big piece right now."

"Cut this pie now?" cried the cook. "No, indeed." Then she laughed. "But I suspected you two might be coming around to tell me good-by." She reached back into the oven and brought out two small saucer pies.

"Here! Watch out you don't burn yourselves."

A whole saucer pie to himself! And it was sweet potato pie, too! Robert decided he liked to say good-by.

The cook didn't seem to feel that way about it at all. "I'm going to miss you boys," she said.

"We'll come back," Smith told her. "Thank you for the pies—and good-by."

"Thank you," Robert repeated after him. "And good-by."

"Now let's go to the stables," said Smith. Away he started. He could walk faster, almost, than Robert could run. Robert still kept wondering why they were saying good-by, but he couldn't talk and run at the same time. It took all of his breath to keep up with his brother.

"Good-morning, Jim," Smith called to the man who took care of the horses. "We've come to say good-by."

Jim seemed as sorry to see them go as the cook had been. He looked so sad Robert tried to cheer him up.

"We'll come back to see you some time. Then you can teach me to ride."

"That I will!" Jim's sad look changed to a grin.

"Father says we children wouldn't be Lees if we didn't love horses," Smith told him.

"That's right," Jim agreed.

"Well, good-by. Come along, Robert. We still have many places to go."

The two boys went from place to place on the big plantation. Robert grew very warm. He was tired of trying to keep up with Smith.

At last even Smith grew hot and tired. He dropped down under a big fig tree to rest. Robert rolled over on the grass by him.

Under the fig tree it was cool and shady. Close by were cornfields, tobacco fields, and cool green woods.

"I think we have said good-by to everybody now," said Smith.

This was Robert's chance. "Why do we have to say good-by, anyway?"

"We are going away tomorrow."

"Why?" Robert brushed off a fly that was buzzing around his nose.

"This house is too big," said Smith. "It is old and shabby, and we have no money to fix it."

Robert looked at the house. It *was* big, and it *was* old and shabby, but it was the only home he had known. He had been born there on January 19, 1807.

"I don't want to go away," he said.

"We have to. If we live in a big house like this, we have to have plenty of horses in the stable. We must have plenty of men to work in the fields. We must have plenty of servants to work in the kitchen and in the house. All of that costs a lot of money. And Father has lost his money."

"Poor Father!" Robert felt very sorry for him.

"Then there is another reason," Smith said. "Carter is twelve years old now. He should be in school. I'm almost big enough to go, too."

"So am I," said Robert, but Smith paid no attention to his remark.

"Only there isn't any school here. There is a good school in Alexandria. Carter can go there. I can go, too. And so can you, when you are big enough."

Robert looked around him. He saw the big fields of corn and the pine woods.

"Are there cornfields in the city?" he asked. He had never seen a city.

"Of course not," said Smith.

"Are there pine-tree woods in the city?"

"No, indeed."

Robert liked the fields and the woods. He wasn't sure what a city would be like, but he was afraid he wouldn't feel at home there. Then he asked one more question. "Will Mother be there?"

"Of course Mother will be there."

"Oh!" said Robert. If Mother was going to be there, everything would be all right.

Along the Way

IT WAS very early the next morning when Robert awoke. It was so early he thought it must still be night. Mammy was shaking him gently.

"Come, come now. It's time to get up."

"I don't want to get up," said Robert sleepily.

Smith was already awake. He grinned at his brother. "Do you want to stay here while the rest of the family goes to Alexandria?"

At the word "Alexandria" Robert was wide awake. He didn't exactly want to leave Stratford, but such a long trip would be exciting. He climbed out of bed and slipped into the clothes that Mammy had ready for him.

"We're going to Alexandria. We're going to Alexandria," he chanted, hopping up and down.

"Hold still, child," said Mammy, "or I'll never fasten these buttons."

A sudden thought struck Robert. He stopped hopping and looked up at Mammy. "We didn't tell you good-by yesterday."

"Of course not. I'm going with you."

"And Nat?" Nat drove the horses.

"Yes, indeed."

Then that was all right. Robert began to jump up and down again.

Just then Mother came to the door. "You had better hurry. It's almost time to start. We'll have to have a quick breakfast."

Breakfast was a strange meal. The children were too excited to eat. The grownups acted as if they weren't hungry.

"I hear the carriage wheels on the drive now," said Mother, and Smith ran to the window. He saw Nat stop the carriage in front of the house. Mammy and other servants began to carry out boxes and bundles. Nat piled them into the carriage.

"I don't believe there will be any room left for us," said Smith. "Anyway, I hope there won't be. Then I can ride on the box with Nat. Maybe he will let me drive."

"I want to drive, too," said Robert. He ran to the window.

At last everyone was ready. Father helped Mother into the carriage.

"You can sit by Mother, Robert," he said. But Robert was running back into the house.

"Where are you going?" Father called. "We're ready to leave."

"I forgot something," Robert called over his shoulder. "Wait for me."

He ran into the nursery and got down on his knees before the empty fireplace. The back of the fireplace was made of iron. It was decorated with two little angels that were made of iron, too. Robert called into the fireplace to them. "Good-by!"

Then he turned and ran back to the carriage.

Everyone except Nat was inside. They were all ready to go.

"You almost got left," Nat told him.

"Come," called Mother.

But Robert held back. "I want to ride on the box with Nat."

"After a while. Not now."

Robert climbed in rather sulkily. Mother made room for him between herself and Ann.

"Don't pout," whispered Ann. "Look! If you lean over my lap, you can wave good-by out the window."

Robert forgot all about being sulky. He leaned over Ann as far as he could. Nat folded up the carriage steps and closed the door. He climbed up into the driver's seat. Now he took the reins in his hands and cracked his whip in the air. The horses moved forward.

Crunch! went the wheels on the road. The Lees were on their way.

The servants came running to the gates. They waved and waved. The Lee children leaned out of the window. "Good-by," they called. "Good-by, everyone, good-by."

PAST WASHINGTON'S HOME

It was a long way from Stratford to Alexandria. The road was very bad. Sometimes it was thick with dust. Sometimes there were deep holes in it.

"This dust is terrible," said Mother. "I do hope our things won't be ruined."

"It hurts my nose!" Robert sneezed.

Just then one of the carriage wheels bumped

into a hole. The carriage swayed, and Robert was jounced right out of his seat. Mother's hat fell off and landed on his head. How they all laughed!

Now the road was smooth. The carriage came to a shallow brook. *Splash! Splash!* The horses waded through the water.

Robert leaned out of the window and looked at the cool woods on each side of the road.

"Look!" he called. "There goes a little squirrel. It ran right in front of the horses!"

"Where?" shouted Smith.

"There it goes up a tree!"

Smith was looking out the other side of the carriage. "I saw a mockingbird!" he called.

"How do you know it was a mockingbird?"

"It had white marks on its wings!"

The carriage rolled on toward Alexandria. The fields of tobacco and corn seemed endless. Soon the boys grew tired.

"I want to do something," said Smith. "Mother, what can we play?"

"I'd rather hear a story," Robert told him.

"Well," Mother said. "I know a true story about something that happened near here. Would you like to hear that?"

"It would be better than a made-up story, any day."

"All right, then. Once upon a time, behind those woods over there, there was a beautiful house called Wakefield."

The boys looked in the direction that Mother was pointing.

"I don't see any house," said Robert.

"Of course not. It burned down years ago."

"Oh!" Robert was disappointed.

"But that isn't part of the story. Now, when Richard Henry Lee was born at Stratford——"

"I know who he was," interrupted Smith. "He was Grandfather's cousin."

"And he was one of the men who signed the Declaration of Independence," Ann added.

"That's right. Now, as I was saying, when Richard Henry Lee was born at Stratford, there was a baby at Wakefield. The baby at Wakefield grew up to be a still more famous man. He was——"

"George Washington!" cried Smith.

"Right you are. And when the babies grew into men, they were the very best of friends."

Smith turned to Father. "George Washington was a friend of yours, too, wasn't he?"

"Indeed he was. He was one of the best friends I ever had."

"And you made a speech about him when he died, didn't you?" asked Smith.

"Yes. I tried very hard to make the kind of speech that he deserved."

"It was a wonderful speech," added Mother. "Father said that George Washington was 'first in war, first in peace, and first in the hearts of his countrymen.' "

"That is a good thing to remember," Ann said.

"Can you say it, Robert?" asked Mother.

Robert tried to say it, and he did very well. It had a nice, jingling sound. The wheels of the carriage seemed to say it, too, as they went around and around.

"First in war, first in peace, and first in the hearts of his countrymen."

Robert had awakened early that morning. Before he knew it, he was fast asleep.

DINNERTIME

The horses kept on and on. The carriage swayed and rocked. Then, after a long, long time, Nat called, "Whoa!" The horses stopped. Robert woke up with a start.

"Are we in Alexandria?" he asked.

"No, sleepyhead," said Father. "It is noon and we are stopping to eat dinner."

Robert and Smith jumped down from the carriage. They had stopped by a little brook that ran across the road. Near by was a big tree with green grass under it.

"Here, Mother," called Smith. "Let's eat under this tree."

Nat drove the horses into the middle of the brook and let them drink. He gave them some oats for their dinner. Then he led them into the shady woods where it was cool. The horses were hot and tired. They needed to rest.

Smith and Robert carried the cushions from the carriage to make a comfortable seat for Mother. She had already begun to open the dinner basket.

"I'll have to give you each an extra big piece of cake for such a nice seat," she told them.

Robert held out his hand eagerly.

"Oh, I didn't mean right away. The cake is for dessert. Here—take a beaten biscuit, each of you, and play until dinner is ready."

Even if it wasn't cake, beaten biscuit was good. Robert munched happily as he ran along with Smith.

Whenever there was any water around, Smith headed for it. In less than no time the boys were by the side of the brook. Smith picked up a dead branch and began to break off twigs.

"Look! I'm making a fleet. You make one, too. We'll sail our boats down the brook."

Soon each boy had enough twigs for a big fleet. They dropped the twigs carefully into the brook. The twigs swirled down the stream. Some of them drifted into quiet little pools, and some caught on snags in the water. But others sailed all the way across the road. Then they disappeared in the underbrush that almost covered the stream on the other side.

"Let's have a boat race," said Smith. "Each of us will put a boat in the water at the same time. Then we'll see which one floats across the road first."

The boys broke off long twigs and threw them into the stream. They ran along the bank as the twigs whirled away.

"Mine's first!" called Smith. But just then his twig caught against a rock that jutted out from the bank. Robert's swept on ahead of it.

"I'm going to win!" shouted Robert. But then his twig started to float over a pebbly place in the bed of the brook. The ripples made by the pebbles turned it in toward the bank.

"No! No!" cried Robert, just as if the twig could understand. "Don't go that way!"

He picked up a dead branch and began to beat the water with it. The waves made the twig turn around. It floated back into the middle of the stream.

Smith grabbed up a branch and splashed away, too. His twig cleared the rock and swirled along after Robert's.

But they never knew which won, because just then Mother called, "Come, boys! Dinner is ready."

They raced back to the big tree.

"Goodness me!" cried Mother. "You're soaking wet, both of you."

Robert was sure she would scold, but Father

stopped her. "Just let them sit in the sun for a while," he laughed. "They'll dry out."

The dinner was as good as Robert had expected it to be. He took two helpings of the sweet potato pie.

"You won't have any room left for that extra big piece of cake," Ann warned him.

But he did. Afterwards, though, he and Smith decided they wouldn't rush back to the brook right away. It was good to lie down under the big tree and look up into the green branches.

It wasn't long, however, before Father was saying, "Come, come, we must be on our way."

ROBERT AND THE HORSES

Soon they were back in the carriage again. The big wheels turned slowly. The carriage bounced and jounced them on their long way once more.

Robert grew tired more quickly this time. Mother was leaning back with her eyes closed. He couldn't ask for another story. Who ever thought such a long trip would be fun, anyway? He wished it was all over and done with.

At last they came to the bottom of a steep hill. Nat reined in the horses.

"Why are we stopping?" Robert asked.

"It is hard for horses to pull a heavy load up a hill," Father told him. "Smith and I will get out and walk up, to make the load lighter."

Nat opened the carriage door and let down the steps. Father and Smith got out.

"I'm going to get out and walk, too," cried Robert.

"The hill is steep," said Mother. "It will be hard to climb."

"Besides," Father added, "you are too small to make much difference to the horses."

"I'm heavy for my age. Mammy says so."

"It will be a long, stiff climb," Father warned. "If you get tired halfway up, Nat can't stop to let you back in the carriage. And you are too big for me to carry."

"I don't want anyone to carry me."

"Well, then—" Father was doubtful, but at last he said, "All right. Come along."

It was a stiff climb, all right. Robert's legs began to grow tired long before they were halfway up. His feet seemed to want to take shorter and shorter steps. But he kept on. He had told Father he could do it, and he would. He was out of breath when he reached the top, but he reached it without even taking his father's hand.

Nat had stopped the horses at the top of the hill. They were resting while they waited for the menfolk of the Lee family to catch up.

"Goodness me!" thought Robert. "The horses must need to rest. It was hard enough for me, and I wasn't pulling a carriage. I'm mighty glad

I could help them. They certainly needed all the help they could get."

Father let down the carriage steps and waited for the boys to climb in.

Smith held back. "I want to ride on the box with Nat."

"So do I," said Robert.

"Well, if Nat doesn't mind——"

"Please, Nat," begged both boys.

Nat looked down at them. He pretended to hesitate. "Do you reckon you can help me hold these horses in?"

"Of course we can!" Robert and Smith cried.

"All right, then. Climb up."

Smith climbed up on the box first. Then Nat reached down to give Robert a helping hand. The two boys settled down by Nat on the high seat.

"All set? Hold on tight!" He cracked his whip in the air. The horses started.

It was even more jouncy up high like this than it had been in the carriage. At first Robert had to hold on tight to Nat on one side and Smith on the other. Soon, though, he began to get his balance. He now could watch the easy sure way in which Nat held the reins.

Nat looked down at him with a grin. "Like to try it?" he asked.

He put the reins in Robert's hands. He held his own big hands over them.

"Look!" cried Robert. "I'm driving! Do the horses know I'm driving?"

"I shouldn't be surprised," said the old man.

"They are stepping mighty carefully," Smith said. "Maybe they know Robert tried to help them, and now they are trying to help Robert."

"It could be," Nat agreed. "It could be."

And on they rode toward Alexandria.

Hello to Alexandria

THE LEE family had been in Alexandria several weeks now. Mammy and Mother had finally decided just where to put each piece of furniture. The family paintings were hung. Even the children had begun to feel at home.

But the house was much smaller than Stratford. The front steps went right down to the sidewalk. There were so many other houses close by that the children had to go a long way before they came to any fields. At first all of them thought that it was fun to sit on the steps and watch wagons and carriages go by. Soon, though, they lost interest.

"Back at Stratford," Ann remembered, "whenever we saw a carriage coming down the lane we ran to call Mother. Here there are so many of them that they make you dizzy."

"They just about make you deaf, too," Smith added, "the way they rattle over the cobblestones."

"Even the river doesn't look the way it did back home." Ann forgot that Alexandria was home now. "Do you remember what the river looked like back there, Robert?"

"It was quiet," said Robert thoughtfully, "and big—and empty."

"That's right." Ann nodded. "Here it is so crowded with ships and boats that their masts make it look like a forest in the wintertime."

Smith jumped up from the steps. "That gives me an idea. Let's go exploring down along the river."

"I can't," said Ann. "Mammy is going to show

me how to make piecrust. But you boys run along."

The two boys raced down toward the river. It wasn't far.

"Ann knew what she was talking about," Smith said. "The wharves are as crowded as the river."

They were too crowded. The bustling men didn't have time to bother with two boys. "Get out of the way," they ordered roughly.

"We'll go on down below the town," Smith decided. "It will be easier to explore down there, anyway."

"Below the town, the river was wide and deep. Far out from the shore, a ship with sails spread was headed toward the bay.

Along the bank grass and weeds grew close to the edge. Sometimes there were trees which leaned out over the water. Their branches dipped into the ripples.

Robert pushed his way under one of the trees.

The branches and the weeds all around the tree made it look almost like a little cave.

"You can't find me!" he called to Smith.

Smith came pushing through. "If you hadn't called out, I never would have known where you were," he said. "This would make a good hideout. Let's keep it a secret."

"Let's."

"The branches are so low we can climb up into the tree, too."

Robert liked that idea. He started up like a squirrel, right away.

"I can see up the river and down the river," he called to Smith. "I can see across it, too."

"Come on down," called Smith. "It's my turn now."

It was harder to climb down than up, but Robert managed to do it without tumbling.

"Now you wait while I climb," said Smith. "Let's play Indian scouts."

44

It was a good game, but finally one of the scouts said, "I'm hungry."

"So am I," said the other. "It must be mighty close to dinnertime."

They crawled out through the bushes. "Let's come back tomorrow," said Smith.

"All right. Let's."

AT THE MARKET

But the next day Father sent Smith on an errand. The boys couldn't go to their hideout. Robert sat on the front steps alone. Sometimes he liked to play by himself, but today he wanted company.

Mother came to the door. She had her hat on and carried her parasol. Behind her came Nat with a big basket. They must be going to market.

At Stratford nearly everything they had had to eat had been grown right on the plantation.

Here in town Mother had to go to market nearly every day. Robert thought it was fun.

He jumped up in a hurry. "I want to go."

"Will you promise not to dawdle—not to poke along and waste time?" asked Mother.

"I never dawdle," said Robert. When his mother laughed, he added, "Well, not very much."

"All right. Just promise not to dawdle very much, and you may go along."

They started off together, but it was hard for Robert to keep his promise. There were too many things to see. Whenever he stopped to look, he kept Mother waiting.

At the very first corner they came to a well. Of course Robert wanted to stop. He ran to the low stone wall that made a curb around the well. He looked over the curb, down into the well. It was deep and dark and shivery. At the very bottom he could see water shining.

"Why is there a well right here on the street?" he asked.

"So that all the people around here can use it," Mother explained.

"Why can't they use the wells in their own yards?"

"Not everyone has a well. Some people have to go a long way for their water. Even then it isn't always good."

"Who dug this well?"

"George Washington had it dug. He had several others dug, too, so that everyone could have good water."

"I wish I could have known George Washington the way Father did."

Mother and Nat started on again toward the market, but Robert stayed behind to watch a Negro woman draw water. She let the bucket down into the well—down, down, until Robert heard it splash. Then she pulled it back up. It was so full it dripped and splashed over the well curb.

She poured the water from the bucket into her pitcher. Then she lifted the pitcher and put it on her head. She held her head so carefully that not a drop of water spilled. Robert watched her go to a house farther down the street.

"I wonder if I could carry a pitcher on my head," thought Robert. He would have liked to try. He would have liked to play, too, in the little puddles the water had made by the well curb.

But Mother was calling, "Robert! You promised not to dawdle."

He ran to catch up with her.

"Now remember," said Mother, "you must stay close to me when we reach the market."

"I shall," said Robert, "but won't you please let me run on ahead now so that I can play just a little while on the old cannon?"

"All right—only wait there for us."

The old cannon had been used in the Revolutionary War. Robert wondered whether George Washington had helped to fire it. Or maybe Father had. The idea sent a tingle of excitement down his back.

He wondered whether the cannon would go off now if anybody put a cannon ball inside. He wondered whether it would be safe to climb up on it. He wondered—but Mother and Nat had caught up with him, and he must start on again.

At last they reached the market place, under the brick arches of the courthouse. The stands there were piled high with fruits and vegetables. Some of the farmers had jogged along country roads all night. They had to reach Alexandria early to get a good place at the market. Now their horses had been led away for food and water. Their carts were backed up against the courthouse wall.

It seemed to Robert that everyone in the market place was talking at once. Many of the people were shouting. They were calling to the shoppers.

"Buy my nice sweet corn!" cried one.

"I've got good fat chickens," called another.

"Watermelons! Nice ripe watermelons!"

Robert started over to the crates of chickens and ducks. As he ran, he almost fell over a pail

of berries. He stepped to the side of the pail and bumped into a basket of eggs.

"Look out, boy!" cried an old man sharply. "Don't you break my eggs!"

Robert managed to keep the basket from turning over. "I'm sorry," he said.

"What are you in such a hurry about?"

"I want to see the chickens and ducks."

"Humph! They won't fly away if you take your time."

"I suppose not."

"It never pays to be in such a rush that you can't see what is right in front of you. Now run along and keep your eyes open."

Robert started back toward Mother. He hoped she hadn't heard the old man scold. She hadn't. She'd been too busy buying corn.

When Nat had put the corn into his basket, Mrs. Lee went on to the old farmer's stand. "I'd like to have two nice chickens."

"Yes ma'am. Here are some good fat ones."

The chickens squawked when the farmer took them out of the crate. He handed them to Nat, who put them in his market basket.

Mother went on to the next cart. Robert followed Nat. He wanted to make sure those chickens didn't get out of the basket. When Nat wasn't looking, he lifted the basket lid and put his hand in to make sure they were still there.

They were. One of them gave him an angry peck on the hand.

"Ouch!" Robert jerked his hand away.

The old farmer had been watching. "That will teach you to keep your hands where they belong," he growled.

"Don't pick on the boy, Pa," the old man's wife said. "Don't you know who he is?"

"I don't know and I don't care."

"He is Light-Horse Harry Lee's son."

"Oh!" The old man looked at Robert more

closely. "No wonder he wasn't scared when I growled."

"It would take more than a cross old farmer to frighten a Lee," his wife agreed.

"That is right." Then the old man spoke to Robert in a much more friendly voice. "Look here, boy. That is a fine old name you have. Make sure you take good care of it."

"Yes, sir," said Robert, but he wasn't at all sure he knew what the farmer meant.

He understood the old man's wife much better when she held out a big basket. "Wouldn't you like to have a pear? They are good and ripe."

Nat had gone on to help Mother, but Robert remembered to say thank you without anyone's reminding him. He dug his teeth into the pear. The sweet juice trickled down his chin.

"Robert!" called Mother, "you *must* stay with me. We're going home now."

Robert ran to catch up again. All the way

home, he stayed close to Mother and Nat. He didn't stop to play. He didn't even eat his pear. He just walked and thought.

When they reached the little brick house, Robert followed Mother into the parlor. "Mother," he asked, "what did that man mean when he said I have a fine old name?"

Mrs. Lee thought for a minute. "It's a little hard to explain. But he meant that for nearly two hundred years the Lees of Virginia have been truthful and honest. They have been gentlemen who could be trusted. They have been fine men—and so their name is a fine name."

"But why did the man say I would have to take care of the name?"

"Because you are a Lee. It's up to you to keep the name of Lee fine. You must be the same kind of person the other Lees have been."

"Oh!" Robert dug his teeth deep down into his pear. Then he said again, "Oh!"

A Game and a Story

THE OLD MAN in the market place was not the only person who knew Father. Many of the soldiers who had been in the army with him came from Alexandria. Some of them still lived there. They liked to tell about the things Light-Horse Harry had done.

Robert and Smith especially liked the exciting story about Father at Paulus Hook.

"The enemy had a strong fort at Paulus Hook during the Revolutionary War," an old soldier told them. "They thought it was so strong it couldn't be taken. But your father and his men crept up very quietly at night.

"They waded in water up to their waists. Suddenly they rushed on the fort and surprised the enemy. The British had to give in."

Robert and Smith made a game out of the story. It was a particularly good game to play by the old cannon. Smith would be Father, and Robert would be one of his soldiers.

"Sir, do you think we can capture the fort?" Robert would whisper.

"Of course," Smith would answer. "I have faith in my men."

They were right in the middle of their game one afternoon when it began to rain.

"We'd better start for home before we get soaked." Smith stopped the game short.

"But we were just about to capture the fort," Robert objected.

"We can play it on the porch just as well as here. Come along!"

Smith started to run. Robert ran, too. As soon

as they reached home they began to pile chairs at one end of the porch to make a fort.

"I'll be Father and you can be the enemy," said Smith.

"All right, but it will be my turn to be Father next time."

Robert crept under the chairs and pretended he was asleep. Smith crawled carefully across the porch toward the chair-fort. When he was very close, he jumped up with a loud yell.

Robert jumped up so quickly that he knocked some of the chairs over. He began to yell, too. Smith tried to drag him out of the fort. Robert tried to drag Smith into it. Soon they were rolling and tumbling over each other all over the porch.

At last Smith was on top. He pinned Robert down to the floor.

"Do you surrender?" he cried.

"Yes, Light-Horse Harry," answered Robert. "And now it is my turn to play Father."

They changed sides and began the game over again. It was a fine game, but it was noisy. They had to admit that. It wasn't long before Ann came to the door.

"Please don't make such a fuss," she said. "The baby has just gone to sleep."

Robert was no longer the youngest child in the Lee family. There was now a baby sister named Mildred.

"I do wish she wouldn't always go to sleep when I want to be noisy, and make such a fuss when I want to go to sleep," sighed Robert.

"Why don't you play a quiet game?" asked Ann.

"We don't like quiet games."

The rain had stopped, but it was too near suppertime to go back to the cannon. The two boys sat down on the steps. They tried to think of something to do that would be fun, but not too noisy.

Robert looked down the street. "Here comes Father!" he cried. "Now we won't need to play any game at all. We'll get Father to tell us a story."

"That sounds good to me," Smith agreed.

The boys ran to meet Father. "Please tell us a story," they begged.

Smith pulled a chair to the side of the porch. "You can sit here and catch the breeze," he said.

"Give me your hat and cane," Robert told Father. "I'll take them into the house."

"You must want that story very much," laughed Father.

"I want to listen, too," said Ann. "Please wait until I get my workbox."

She went inside to get her sewing. There was never any end to the sewing in the Lee family. Every dress, and even Father's suits, had to be made by hand. Today, Ann was stitching some ruffles for Father's neckcloth.

The boys were sitting on the porch steps when she came back. She sat down beside them.

"Now you can begin," she said.

"We want a story about the war," said Robert.

"With a woman in it," Ann added.

"Women don't fight," Robert objected.

"But they love their country just the same as men do, don't they, Father?"

"Of course they do. It isn't enough just to fight for your country. You must love it enough to be ready to give up anything you have if your country needs it."

"Women can do that," said Ann.

"I know one woman who did," Father agreed.

A GOOD STORY

"The woman's name," Father began, "was Mrs. Motte. Before the Revolutionary War, she lived in a beautiful home on a hill.

"Then the enemy came. They thought her home would make a good fort. They took it away from her. Her husband was dead, and she had no one to help her. She had no place to go except to a very small house over on the next hill."

"Poor Mrs. Motte!" said Ann.

"But you got her house back for her, didn't you, Father?" asked Robert.

Father shook his head. "I tried to."

"What happened?"

"I was sure we could drive the enemy out, if we could get our soldiers up close to the house before we were fired on," said Father. "We left men back on the road to watch. Then we began to dig a deep ditch. We thought we could creep up to the house through the ditch.

"But suddenly one of the men who had been left on guard came dashing up from the road. He called that there were many British soldiers coming. They would be upon us in a very short time."

Robert shivered. "What did you do?"

"We had to capture the fort before they arrived. If we didn't, we would have the new soldiers on one side of us and the men in the fort on the other."

"Then you would be shot to pieces," Smith declared.

"We surely would. There was only one thing to do. Instead of helping Mrs. Motte get her house back, we would have to burn it down."

"How terrible!" cried Ann.

"Yes. She had been very kind to us. I hated to tell her what we were going to do. But when I did, what do you think she did?"

"She begged you not to burn the house down."

"She did not. She said she would be glad to have her big house burned, if burning it would help her country.

"She went back into her little house. She brought us a bow and some arrows. We set fire to one of the arrows and shot it into the roof of her fine old home. The sun had dried the roof, and it caught fire quickly.

"We shot a second blazing arrow and then a third. Soon the whole roof was on fire. The enemy had to come out. We took them prisoners. But Mrs. Motte's beautiful home was burned to the ground."

"What did she do then?" asked Robert.

"She invited as many of us to dinner as her little house would hold."

"She was a real patriot," said Robert.

"Yes, son," said Father. "She was."

"I Am a Soldier's Son!"

IT DID seem as if a man who knew the fine stories Father did ought to tell his children one every day. But the longer the Lees lived in Alexandria, the busier Father seemed to be. There were men coming to see him. There were men he must go to see. Besides, he always had long, long letters to write. He had very little time to be with his children.

At last, though, there came a sunny afternoon when the boys were playing in the yard.

"Oh, there you are," said Father. "I was just going to hunt you up. Would you like to take a walk down to the river?"

They certainly would.

"Maybe he will tell us a story on the way," Robert whispered to Smith.

But he didn't. He didn't have a chance even to begin one. He had to stop to speak to this person and then to that one. Father was a very popular man in Alexandria.

"Maybe, after we get to the river——"

They never reached the river. They had hardly gone halfway when they met a man riding a big bay horse. He pulled the horse up short when he saw Father. He seemed excited.

"I was on my way to your house," he said. "I have just come back from Baltimore."

"Did you see Hanson?" Father asked.

"I did, indeed." The man got down from his horse. He and Father began to talk.

Robert and Smith were more interested in the horse than they were in the man. They walked all around her and told each other her good points. Finally, though, they grew tired of waiting for Father. They'd never reach the river if the man kept him there talking all afternoon.

"Besides, it isn't good for Father to get so excited," Smith whispered. "Mother says so. See how red his face is."

"Look how he is pounding with his cane," Robert whispered back. "He is certainly angry at something or somebody."

"I tell you, Sir," Father was almost shouting, "no man should ever give way to a mob."

"I agree," said the man, "but what are we going to do about it?"

"I'll tell you what we can do about it."

Father lowered his voice, and the two men went on talking. At last Father's friend got back on his horse and rode away.

"Good!" whispered Smith. "Now maybe we can get started again."

But Father had other ideas. "Rightabout-face, boys," he said. "It's back home for us, and in double quick time, too. I must get ready to go to Baltimore in the morning."

They headed back home. Father was still excited. He hit out with his cane at the weeds that grew by the edge of the road. It must be the thought of that mob that made him so angry.

"Father!" asked Robert, "what is a mob?"

"It is a crowd of people who get so angry and excited that they do cruel, wicked things. A mob won't listen to anybody. Sometimes people are killed before a mob can be stopped."

"A mob would listen to *you*, wouldn't it?" Robert asked proudly. "It would know you were George Washington's friend. It would remember how you fought in the Revolutionary War."

Father shook his head. "People in a mob don't remember things like that. But you boys must always remember—never give in to a mob."

They had reached home and were opening the door in the hall.

"Run now and call Mammy," said Father. "Tell her I have to start packing."

BAD NEWS

The next morning Father left for Baltimore. The family stood at the door to wave good-by to him. Mammy had Baby Mildred in her arms. Robert reached for her hand and made her wave good-by, too.

Nearly a week passed by. It was such good weather the boys went down to their secret hideout nearly every morning. Each one of them had a favorite lookout place in the old tree now. Sometimes they played that they were Indians and at other times that they were sailors. But always by dinnertime they were boys again, in a hurry to get home.

"Look," said Smith as they ran into the yard one day. "There is a horse tied to the hitching post."

Robert recognized the horse at once. "It is the bay that man was riding the day we didn't get to take a walk with Father."

"I wonder what that man is doing here."

The boys ran into the house. Ann was standing in the hall. She was looking first at a big white hat on the hall table, then at the closed door to the parlor. It was plain that she was wondering, too, what the visitor was doing there.

"Who is he?" Smith whispered.

"I don't know," Ann answered.

"What is he here for?"

"I don't know that, either. Mammy says that when she opened the door, the man said, 'I must speak with Mrs. Lee at once.' He has been in there nearly half an hour now. And I am almost sure I heard Mother crying."

The children looked at each other. They felt they ought to do something, but they didn't know exactly what.

Finally the parlor door opened. Mother and the man came out. Ann was right. Mother had been crying.

But she held herself stiff and straight as she said good-by to her visitor. She watched while he got on his horse and rode away. Then she turned to the children.

"Your father has been badly hurt," she said. Her voice wasn't quite steady.

"How?" asked Ann.

Robert remembered his talk with Father. "Was it a mob?" he asked.

Mother nodded her head.

"Is the man on the bay horse going to bring him home?"

"Not yet," said Mother. "He won't be able to travel for a while."

Mammy came to the door. "Your dinner is getting stone-cold," she fussed.

"Mammy!" Robert ran to her. "Father has been hurt by a mob!"

"Tch! Tch!" Mammy put her arm around Mother as if she were a little girl. "Don't you fret. He's going to get well."

"What happened?" Robert asked Mother. "Did the man tell you?"

"As much as he knew. Your father's friend, Mr. Hanson, is a newspaper editor. Some people didn't like what he printed. They threatened to burn his house down if he didn't stop."

"And Father said he should never give in to a mob," Robert remembered.

"Yes. Your father was positive about that. He went to Baltimore to help his friend.

"The mob came again. The angry crowd set fire to the building where the newspaper presses were. Men tried to attack Mr. Hanson's house."

"But Father was there!" cried Robert. "He held the mob back!"

"For a while—yes. Several other friends were there, too. They held the house as if it were a fort. But the mob was yelling and howling. There were dozens of men out there for each man in the house. At last they forced their way in. They grabbed your father and his friends and beat them."

"But Father is going to get well, isn't he?"

"I hope so. Oh, I hope so!"

"Of course he is going to get well," said Mammy. "Don't you worry yourself about that."

ANOTHER GOOD-BY

It was a long time before Father's friends brought him home. He looked very pale. He wasn't even able to walk. All day long he lay in his big bed.

74

There was a lot of work to be done with an invalid in the house. Robert soon found that out. He ran errands for Mother. He took his turn tending the baby so that Mammy could help nurse Father.

"Here, Mildred," said Robert. "If you will stop crying, I'll let you play with my ball."

For a few moments Mildred was satisfied. Then she started to cry again.

"Please, Mildred," said Smith. "You'll bother Father. Wouldn't you like to play with my nice, brown horse chestnuts?"

Finally Mildred, as well as the boys, learned to play very quietly. But Father didn't get any better.

"Pst!" whispered Smith to Robert one afternoon. "I have something to tell you."

"What is it?"

"Come down to the hideout."

They hurried down to the river. They climbed to their lookout places.

"Now, what is it?" asked Robert.

"I heard the doctor talking with Mother. He said Father isn't getting any better here, and he ought to go to some hot sunny place in the South."

"Will he get better there?"

"Maybe. But the doctor certainly did look worried."

Robert looked out over the river. Of course, he hadn't seen Father very much since he'd been brought back home, but he knew they all would be very, very lonesome without him.

"Still, if it will make him well, I reckon we can stand it," he decided.

Just a few days later, the Lee children stood in the hall to tell Father good-by.

"You must take good care of Mother while I am away," he told them. "I'll be back just as soon as I can."

Nat helped Father into the carriage.

"Good-by! Good-by!" called the children.

The horses started. Soon the carriage rounded a bend in the road. Then it was out of sight.

Mother and Ann were crying. Robert wanted to cry, too, but he didn't.

"I am a soldier's son," he told himself. "A soldier's son must act like a soldier."

Stay-at-Home Schoolboy

THE ACADEMY was a school for big boys. Carter had been going there ever since the Lees had moved to Alexandria. Not long after Father went away, Smith started to go there, too.

"I want to go with you," Robert begged.

"You can't. You're too young. Besides, you have to learn to read first. You must learn to write, too, and to work sums on your slate."

"Why can't I learn all that at school with you?"

"The teacher hasn't time to bother with younger boys. Besides, Mother can teach you at home just as well. That is the way most of the boys around here start."

"Oh!" Robert was still sure it would be more fun to learn at school than at home.

He felt better, though, after he had talked with Mother. "With the other boys away all day," she said, "I don't know how I could get along without you." That made him feel needed.

It was good, too, to be able to play a little while longer, each morning, after the other boys had started off to school.

As soon as breakfast was over, Nat brought a small tub of hot water into the dining room. He put it on the table in front of Mother. She carefully washed the silver teapot, the sugar dish, and the thin cups and saucers. These dishes were too precious to be sent to the kitchen. While she was busy, Robert ran outdoors for a last romp with his dog, Spec.

"Only don't go too far away," Mother warned him. "I want you to put in full time on your lessons today."

Robert ran out into the chilly morning. Spec was waiting for him. "Come here, Spec," he called. "I bet you can't catch me."

The boy and his dog chased up and down the yard together. Several times Robert stopped and let Spec knock him down. The two of them rolled over and over each other.

Then Robert threw a stick and Spec brought it back, but he wouldn't give it up. He held on to one end while Robert pulled on the other. It was a grand tug of war.

All too soon, though, Mother called. "Robert! It is time to come in, now."

Spec trotted up to the door with him.

"You stay right here," Robert told the dog. "I'll be back just as soon as I can."

Spec wagged his tail. Then he curled up by the door.

Robert went inside. He hung up his cap and went on into Mother's room.

It was a cool morning. Nat had built a fire in the big open fireplace. Mother was sitting by the fire. She was knitting a stocking for Smith.

"I wish I didn't have to learn to read," said Robert.

"Many boys never do learn," Mother answered quietly. "They just play outdoors all day long."

"Then why can't I?"

Mother didn't answer the question. "And when they grow up," she went on, "they are just like Old John. Do you know Old John?"

Robert nodded. "He lives down by the river. He spends all his time fishing and hunting. But his cabin is old, and the roof leaks. His clothes are old and shabby, too."

"And he has never learned to read and write," Mother added. "When he wants to sign his name, he has to make an X and then have somebody else write by it, 'John—his mark.'"

"Oh!" Robert sighed.

"Of course, if you want to grow up to be like him——"

Robert didn't wait for her to finish her sentence. He ran to the candlestand for his reader.

"Come, sit here," said Mother. She pushed a footstool close by the fire.

Robert sat down. He opened his book. It had only a few pictures. The print was very small.

The pages were fastened together so tightly that it was hard to hold the book open. The cover was made of thin, wooden boards. These were covered with blue paper.

On the first page of this blue-backed speller there was a picture of George Washington. The next page showed the letters of the alphabet.

"Now point to the letters with this pin," said Mother, "and tell me what they are."

Robert pointed with his pin. "Big A, little a," he said. "Big B, little b." He went on through the whole alphabet.

"Good!" said Mother. "Now we can start on the next page."

The next page was filled with rows of letters put together.

ab eb ib ob ub

ac ec ic oc uc

"They don't make any sense."

"They don't," Mother agreed. "But you must

learn them before you can begin to spell words. Then I'll be sure you know your letters."

She pointed with her knitting needle to the first line.

"A—b," said Mrs. Lee, "ab."

"A—b," Robert said after her, "ab."

It wasn't very interesting.

"Have children always had to start with a book like this?" he asked.

"No," said Mother. "Not so long ago most children used what were called hornbooks. But they weren't really books at all."

"What were they then?"

"Well, a hornbook looked something like a hand-mirror. It had just such a handle. But instead of the mirror, there was a piece of paper.

"On the paper were printed the letters of the alphabet and the Lord's Prayer. The paper was covered by a piece of horn."

"What was that for?"

"It was so thin that you could see through it. It kept the paper from getting dirty or torn, you see.

"Then there was a hole in the handle for a piece of string. The owner could hang the horn-book around his neck or tie it around his waist."

Robert laughed. "It must have looked funny to see children running around with their horn-books hanging down from their waists."

Mother smiled, too. "I heard of a teacher once," she said, "who made letters of gingerbread for her pupils. Then, when the children had learned their letters, they could eat their lesson."

Ann came into the room just as Mother was talking about gingerbread.

"I came past the kitchen just now," she said. "Maybe it wasn't gingerbread letters I smelled, but I think it was right good gingerbread, just the same. It smelled as if it would be done by the time you finish your lesson."

Robert picked up his book again in a hurry.

"E—b, eb," said Mother.

"E—b, eb," repeated Robert.

The lesson was finished very quickly. Then Robert jumped up and ran to the kitchen. In almost no time at all, he was out in the yard.

"Here, Spec!" he called. He held up a big piece of gingerbread.

Spec jumped for it. Then they ran down to the stable.

A VISIT TO ARLINGTON

They found Nat harnessing the horses.

"Where are you going?" Robert asked.

"To Arlington. I have to take a letter to Mrs. Custis. If I knew a boy who promised to mind very well, I might take him with me."

"I'm that boy!" cried Robert.

"Is your mother willing?"

Robert ran back to the house. "Mother!" he called. "Nat says he'll take me to Arlington if you will let me go."

"Go ahead," Mother called back.

Robert ran to get ready. Baby Mildred began to cry. She wanted to go, too.

"You mustn't cry," Robert told her. "You can't go, because you'd get too tired and cold. But when I come back, I'll bring you a present."

Mildred stopped crying. Robert called good-by to Mother and climbed up on the box. Nat slapped the reins over the horses' backs. Away they went.

The air was so cold that Robert's fingers tingled. He clapped his hands together to warm them.

"I reckon Jack Frost came last night," said Nat. "He can bite a body's fingers almost off. There is something else he can do, too."

He pointed to a sweet gum tree by the side of

the road. All summer long its leaves had been green. Now they were bright red.

"Oh, stop, Nat!" cried Robert. "Let me get some leaves. They will make a good present for Mildred."

Nat didn't stop. "Just you wait," he said. "I'll show you a nicer present than that. Jack Frost has fixed it just right for Miss Mildred."

"What is it?" asked Robert.

Nat shook his head. "Just you wait."

Robert was puzzled for a little while, but soon he forgot all about it. He was very busy enjoying everything he saw.

They drove past fields where the grass was stiff with frost. Along the Potomac River the wild ducks were bobbing up and down with the ripples on the water.

At last the carriage came to a steep hill. On the top of the hill stood a large house.

"Arlington is as big as Stratford," said Robert.

"Yes," Nat replied, "but Stratford doesn't have big pillars like the ones at the front of this house."

They drove up the hill and stopped in front of the big pillars. Then they climbed down from the carriage. Nat lifted the brass knocker on the door of the house. Soon a Negro servant opened the door. He took the letter Nat handed him.

Just then Mary Custis came hurrying to the door. She was about as old as Robert. They were very good friends.

"You must come in and get warm," she told Nat. "Oh, and there is Robert! Both of you must come in."

Nat went to the kitchen to warm his feet before the big kitchen fire. Robert followed Mary into the hall.

She waited while he warmed his fingers and toes.

"It is such a frosty morning, we weren't expect-

ing any company," Mary said, "but I certainly am glad to see you. Are you warm enough now? Then what shall we do first? Mother says I must always let 'company' choose what we shall do. What game do you want to play?"

Robert's mother always told him the same thing. When Mary came to his house, he had to play what she chose. He was glad that he was the one to be 'company' today. There was something special he wanted to do.

"I don't want to play any game at all," he said. "I'd like to look at George Washington's things."

Mary's father was George Washington's stepson. She was as proud of being the granddaughter of the First President of the United States as Robert was of being Light-Horse Harry's son. There was nothing she would rather do than show visitors the belongings of her famous grandfather.

"Here is one of my grandfather's uniforms,"

Mary said proudly. "Would you like to hold it a minute? Then, if you'd like, I'll show you the cups and saucers that used to be his, and the bed he slept in."

Robert was enjoying himself so much he would have liked to stay all day. It wasn't long, though, before Mrs. Custis called him. "Nat is ready to leave, Robert. He says your mother is waiting for my answer to her letter."

Robert took a last look around him. "I'll come back another day," he said to himself.

Then he said aloud, "I'm coming."

THE PRESENT

Mary stood at the door and waved good-by.

"That's a mighty fine little lady," said Nat.

"Um-hum," said Robert, but he wasn't very much interested in girls. He was still thinking about George Washington.

Then, suddenly, he remembered something. "Oh, Nat!" he cried, "we haven't found the present for Mildred yet."

"Don't fret," said the old man. "Just you wait."

They rode along for quite a way. At last they came to a clump of trees.

"I reckon," Nat said, "you might find her a present in there. While you're hunting one way, I'll be hunting another."

"What do I look for?" asked Robert.

"You'll know when you find it."

Nat stopped the horses. He and Robert climbed down.

"You go that way and I'll go this," said Nat. "Keep your eyes open."

Robert started into the woods. "How can I find a present when I don't know where to look?" he asked himself.

He looked at the tops of the tall trees. Some of the leaves had started to fall. He shuffled his

feet through the dead leaves on the ground. Still he did not find the present.

Then he saw some very small trees. Or were they large bushes? Robert didn't stop to decide, for they were filled with prickly burs, and each bur was opened to show a small brown nut. It looked like a little chestnut.

"Hurrah!" shouted Robert. "Chinkapins!"

He popped one into his mouth. The shell was so thin that he could bite into it with his teeth. He ate it quickly. Then he bit into another.

94

"Nat was right!" he told himself. "Yesterday the burs were closed tight. But Jack Frost opened them during the night."

He began to gather chinkapins as fast as he could. His cap was nearly full when Nat came back.

Nat was excited, too. "What do you think I saw?" he asked. "A wild turkey! Yes, sir, a turkey! I'm going home to get my gun. If your mother will let me stop work, I'll go hunting. How would you like to have turkey for dinner tomorrow?"

Mildred was taking her nap when Nat and Robert reached home. Robert showed the chinkapins to Ann and explained that he had brought them for Mildred.

"Fine!" said Ann. "But we mustn't give them to the baby like that. She would put them into her mouth and swallow them whole. Wait a minute."

Ann got a sharp needle. She threaded it with a strong thread. Then she strung the chinkapins on the thread.

"There! Now we'll see what Miss Mildred thinks of that. Listen! She's waking up now."

Robert ran to Mildred's crib. The little girl was just sitting up. He put the chinkapin necklace over her head. The baby was delighted.

"It is a fine present," Mother said.

"Part of it is from me," said Robert, "and part from Nat, and part from Jack Frost."

"Didn't you bring me a present?" Ann teased.

"I brought you something better," said Robert.

"What is it?"

"I brought you a secret," Robert said. He came close and whispered in her ear, "We are going to have wild turkey for dinner tomorrow. Nat and I are going hunting."

A New Song
Is Born

THE WAR of 1812 with England had been going on for more than a year. Carter had explained what it was about to Smith. Smith explained it to Robert. Robert tried to explain it to little Mildred. Mildred, though, was too young to understand, or even to listen.

"We are going to win," Robert told her. "Just you wait and see. England hasn't any right to take our sailors and make them work on her ships. She hasn't any right to stop all our ships and search them."

Mildred looked up at him with a smile. "Play horse?" she asked.

"You ought to listen to me," Robert insisted. "Can you remember our half brother, Harry Lee? He's ever so much older even than Carter is. He is a grown man, and Stratford belongs to him now. Well, he's in the army fighting for America."

Mildred climbed into Robert's wagon. "Play horse now," she said firmly.

Robert gave in. Ann had knitted some reins for Mildred to use when Robert played horse with her. Robert put them under his arms and handed Mildred the ends.

"Giddy-up!" cried Mildred. She slapped the reins. Robert picked up the tongue of the wagon. He raced around the room. He stamped his feet like a horse on the bare floor. He made such a big noise that Mildred laughed aloud.

Boom! Boom! came a loud noise from outside the house. Robert stopped short.

"Mother!" he called. "What was that?"

Mildred was frightened. She dropped the reins. Mother came hurrying through the hall.

"It is the cannon!" she cried. "There must be news of some battle!"

"Have we won?" asked Robert.

"I don't know."

Other women and children were running down the street. Robert ran with them.

A young man came racing toward them. He waved his hat and shouted as he ran.

"Hurrah!" he cried. "Hurrah!"

"What is the news?" cried Robert.

" 'We have met the enemy and they are ours!' "

"Where? When? Who?"

Everybody was shouting at once. The people crowded around the man. He was so out of breath he could hardly talk.

"Hold on!" he gasped. "I can't tell you a thing if you keep asking questions."

The crowd quieted down.

"The news has just arrived," said the man. "Lieutenant Oliver Hazard Perry has led his men in a battle with the British fleet on Lake Erie. He has sent the message, 'We have met the enemy and they are ours!' "

The people shouted. Down the street the cannon boomed.

The young man started off again. Robert ran along beside him. Smith joined them.

100

"Hurrah!" they called to everybody they saw. " 'We have met the enemy and they are ours.' "

Both boys were tired when they got back home, but they were still excited. They raced up the front steps and into the house.

"As soon as I'm old enough I'm going to join the Navy," said Smith. "I'm going to be a hero like Lieutenant Perry. Heroes always win."

"No, they don't. Do they, Mother?" said Robert.

"Not always," Mother agreed. "Do you remember Captain Lawrence? Last summer he commanded a ship in a battle with the British near the city of Boston."

"He was killed," Smith remembered, "but his last words were 'Don't give up the ship.' "

"He died fighting," Robert added.

"Was he a hero?" asked Mother.

Smith's answer was quick and sure. "Of course he was."

"He didn't win," said Mother gently.

Both boys thought about that for a moment. "Captain Lawrence was brave, though, and he did his very best," Robert said at last.

Mother nodded. "That is what makes a true hero," she said.

THE WAR COMES CLOSE

Another year went by. Sometimes the war was so far away that Robert almost forgot about it. When summer came again, though, he found that it was very real.

Just a few miles across the Potomac River from his home was the city of Washington. It was the very new and very beautiful capital of the United States.

That summer the British began to march on Washington. Every day they came nearer and nearer.

Very soon they were on their way.

The snow was melting. Already there were bare spots in the fields. The melted snow filled the holes in the road with water. The road became muddy.

The wheels of the carriage sank deep into the mud. The horses tugged with all their strength, but almost as soon as they were out of one hole they landed in another. At last they came to one bigger than any of the others. The wheels of the carriage stuck!

Nat climbed down from the box.

"You boys had better climb out and help him," said Mother.

The boys went into the woods with Nat. There they cut some small trees.

"We'll use these for poles," said Nat.

The boys dragged them down to the road. Nat got down on his knees to shove them under the carriage in front of the wheels.

"Now, stand back. We'll try again."

The boys stood back. The horses pulled and tugged once more. Slowly, they drew the wheels up through the sucking mud until they rested on the firm tree trunks.

They were out of the hole at last.

It was late when the Lee family arrived at the Fitzhughs' home. Most of the other guests were already there. It seemed to Robert as if there were dozens and dozens of them. "I'd forgotten we had so many cousins and uncles and aunts," he whispered to Smith. "I wonder whether there will be beds enough for us all."

There weren't. Already in the boys' room the servants were putting mattresses on the floor and covering them with sheets and blankets.

Smith grinned. "I bet, tomorrow night, we'll have some fun, with all of us boys in one room. Tonight, though, if the others are as tired as I am——"

114

"I reckon they are," Robert decided reasonably. "They came over the same roads that we did."

He was right. Most of the boys were too worn out even to say good night. Ten minutes after the candles were blown out, the whole roomful of boys was asleep.

GETTING READY

The next morning, though, they were up as early as anyone else in the house. It was the day before Christmas. Who wanted to lie abed?

As soon as they had had breakfast, the boys went racing outdoors.

"Come along!" called someone down by the barn. "The wagon is ready. We're off to get the Christmas greens."

It was always the young people who gathered the Christmas greens. Boy cousins, girl cousins, young lady and young men cousins—all of them started off to the woods in the big wagon.

At last they came to a place where the holly trees grew thick. Running cedar trailed over the ground.

Robert and his cousins gathered great armloads of the running cedar. They broke off branches of holly.

"Hey, Smith, is that you?" Robert called. Smith was carrying such a large load of cedar that only his feet and arms could be seen.

The wagon was so full there was no room for the cousins to get back in. They had to walk along behind. Soon they came to the little country church.

"We'll put holly in the windows first," Ann called.

While the girls filled each window with the green branches, the boys brought a ladder. They hung the running cedar along the walls.

Then all of them stood back to look.

"It is really beautiful," they decided.

Outside, some of the boys climbed back into the wagon.

"Where are you off to, now?" called Ann.

"Back to the woods to get a new load. It is going to take a lot of holly to trim Cousin William's ballroom and the big hall."

"We'll meet you at the house, then."

The wagon was soon filled a second time. Once more the boys had to walk behind.

Cousin William's stableman, who was driving the mules, had a son just about Robert's age. He had brought him along to help with the mules and to enjoy the fun.

Now the boy ran up to Robert. "Look!" He pointed up into a big tree.

Robert looked up into the tree. The leaves were gone. Through the bare branches he could see a thick clump of something near the top.

"It is just an old bird's nest filled with leaves," he said.

"Look again!"

Then Robert whistled. "Mistletoe!"

"Yes sirree," said the boy. "I'll get it!"

He put his arms around the tree. Then he dug his knees and feet into the thick bark. The next minute he was climbing up the tree like a squirrel.

118

Robert stood underneath the tree and waited until the boy reached the mistletoe.

"Ready?" called the boy.

"I'm right here."

"Here it comes!" the boy cried. He dropped the mistletoe right into Robert's hands. Then he scampered down from the tree.

The two boys ran after the others.

"Hi-yi!" they called. "Mistletoe!"

Everybody laughed.

"That is just what we need," one of the young men cousins declared. "It wouldn't be Christmas without a piece of mistletoe hanging in the hall."

"Good for you, Robert!" another one said. "Which of the girls are you going to catch under your mistletoe?"

Everyone knew that if you caught a girl under the mistletoe, you could kiss her.

"It isn't my mistletoe," Robert said hastily. "It is his." He pointed to the boy.

"Besides," Smith teased, "Robert's sweetheart isn't here. She lives in——" Then he ducked. Robert had thrown a pine cone at him.

"Here," one of the big cousins told the stableman's son. "Robert says it is your mistletoe. I'll give you a dollar for it."

He gave the boy a big silver dollar. The boy ran ahead to show his money to his father.

As soon as the wagon reached the big house, the hurrying and scurrying began all over again. One or two last-minute guests had arrived. They laughed at the way everyone was hustling.

"What is all the rush about?" they asked. "Haven't you got all the rest of the day to get things ready?"

Robert stopped on his way into the hall with a big rope of cedar. "No, indeed," he answered. "The servants are having a dance tonight at the barn. And then there will be the fireworks. And then——"

"Where is that cedar?" someone in the hall called out.

Robert rushed on with his load.

It was dinnertime before the last holly wreath was made and hung.

"There!" sighed one of the girls. "We've finished."

Everyone stood back to look. "It really is beautiful," they decided.

"And I really am hungry," said Robert.

"ISN'T CHRISTMAS FUN?"

But even though it was almost dinnertime, Robert still had a while to wait. There were so many guests the dining room wouldn't hold them all at once. The grown people went in to the first table. The children had to wait for the second.

"It won't be too long, though," Robert told

121

Smith. "Mother is mighty anxious to get back upstairs to finish all the last-minute things, and I reckon most of the other mothers feel the same way. They won't sit around and talk in the dining room."

"And the menfolk are all anxious to get at the fireworks. They won't fire them off until night, but they want to unpack everything and get ready."

"As soon as we finish eating, let's see if they will let us help."

But they didn't have time. It was already dark when the children left the table. Lights were twinkling down at the barn.

"We don't want to miss seeing the first dance!" They raced off.

Down in the barn the musicians were tuning up. One man played a banjo. Another had his homemade fiddle. Soon they struck up a jig-tune. Two or three men ran out into the middle of the floor. They began to jig—slowly at first, then faster and faster. They jumped into the air. They hit their heels together.

Everyone began to stamp in time with the music and to clap. Robert and his friends clapped and stamped, too. At last the musicians stopped. They were out of breath themselves. They mopped their faces with their handkerchiefs. But they couldn't rest very long. Someone called for a reel.

Robert felt he could watch them all night, but suddenly there came a loud *Bang!* from up near the big house. The fireworks were starting.

The boys left the barn in a hurry. They raced back to the big house. Out on the lawn the men had stacked their fireworks on a long table. Now they were setting them off.

The women and children stood at the doors and windows watching. They put their hands over their ears when a big firecracker went off.

They clapped when the skyrockets went high up in the air, then dropped their golden stars.

Robert ran up to his mother. "Where is Mildred? She ought to see this."

"She is fast asleep—where you should be."

"Not on Christmas Eve!"

"Well—" Mother laughed. "All right. Not on Christmas Eve."

Robert ran back to the lawn. Someone gave him a Roman candle to shoot off. Smith had some torpedoes. Robert felt as if he had never heard such noise or had more fun.

It was late before the boys went to bed. No wonder they slept soundly. They never saw what went on during the rest of the night, nor when it happened.

But the next morning the stockings which they had left at the foot of their beds were filled. Each boy in the room had one. Excitedly the cousins called to one another.

"Look! Gloves!"

"I have a whistle."

"See my knife!"

Candy and nuts and apples were rolling out of the stockings all over the beds.

"I don't believe I need a really big breakfast today," said Smith. He had just popped a big piece of candy into his mouth.

"No," grinned Robert. "I don't believe I do, either. Just two or three eggs and some waffles and bacon and spoonbread—just enough to last until dinnertime."

As soon as breakfast was over, it was time to start to church. Some people drove over in the carriages. Others rode horseback. Robert and Smith walked with the other boys.

"What are you carrying?" Smith asked. He looked at the queer iron box Robert was swinging by its handle as he walked.

"A footstove Cousin William lent me. It is

126

full of good hot coals. They'll keep Mother's feet warm no matter how cold it is in church."

The church looked very beautiful with all of its green trimmings. The cedar filled it with a Christmas odor.

Robert knelt with his family while they prayed. The Christ Child seemed very near.

The walk back in the cold air gave everyone a good appetite for dinner. But this time the children had to wait a long, long time. It seemed as if the older people would never get their fill of turkey and plum pudding.

At last, though, it was time for the women to dress for the ball. They started upstairs. The children streamed into the dining room.

One of the turkeys had been saved especially for them. Robert got the wishbone. He pulled it with Smith.

"I got the curved part!" Robert cried. "My wish is going to come true!"

The candles in the ballroom and in the hall had been lighted by the time the children left the dining room.

"Your mother is looking for you, Robert," someone told him.

"And I am looking for Mother," said Robert.

He met her on the stairs. "Mother," he began, "you are going to let us sit up until the ball begins, aren't you?"

"That is what I wanted to talk with you about," said Mother. "If I let you sit up through the first dance, will you promise to go to bed quickly then, without bothering anybody?"

"Yes, ma'am!"

"Well, then——"

"I got my wish!" cried Robert. "I wished on the wishbone that you would let us stay up."

Most of the other mothers were getting their children to promise the same thing. Robert ran to join his cousins on the big wide stairs.

"We've saved a place for you," someone called. "You can see everything here."

Just then there was a loud sound from the brass knocker on the front door. Pompey, the butler, opened the door wide. There was a flurry of wind that set all the hall candles to winking. In came a group of men and women.

The ladies started upstairs to take off their hoods and cloaks. The children squeezed together to make room for them to pass. The men

went into Cousin William's library to warm themselves. They were back at the foot of the steps, though, when the ladies came down. They went together into the ballroom.

Now the musicians were beginning to play. "Listen," whispered Ann. "A minuet."

The children looked through the big doors into the ballroom. The men were bowing to their partners.

"I do hope the minuet is a long dance," Robert whispered back.

It was over all too soon. The children started upstairs very, very slowly. Nobody wanted to go, but a promise was a promise.

"Besides," Smith admitted, "I don't believe I am going to need anyone to rock me to sleep."

"Nor I," Robert said. "I can hardly keep my eyes open." He slipped between the sheets of his mattress bed and pulled the covers up to his chin. "But isn't Christmas fun?"

Two Visits

SPRINGTIME was kite time. Every boy in Alexandria knew that. But it was the time for quick, hard showers, too.

Robert and two of the neighborhood boys had been playing in the yard. A heavy shower had driven them into the house. Now they stood looking out the window. Rain was pouring down. Out in the yard the wet bushes were waving their new-green branches in the wind.

"Let's make ourselves a kite," said Robert.

"What sense is there in making a kite?" asked one of the boys. "It is against the law to fly kites in the streets of Alexandria."

"My goodness, why?" asked Robert.

"You might scare the horses."

"That is silly," said the other boy. "But horses don't have much sense, for a fact."

"Yes they do!" Robert loved horses. He was always ready to stick up for them. "Horses have more sense than human beings do, sometimes. And I bet you would be scared, too, if you had on blinders that kept you from seeing anywhere but straight in front of you, and suddenly something big and floppy fell out of the air and hit you on the head!"

"Maybe I might at that!" They all laughed.

"Anyway, we could make a kite and fly it in a field outside the city," Robert insisted.

But by this time the rain was over. The sun was peeping out from the clouds as if he were ashamed of having been a runaway himself.

"It is too much work to make a kite," said one of the boys. "Come on. Let's play leapfrog."

Robert played leapfrog, but he still wanted his kite. That evening, after supper, he began to make one.

He started with a long, thin stick, and a short one. He tied them together in the shape of a long cross. He took some string that he had been saving and fastened it at the top end of the long stick. Then he carried the string on to one of the ends of the crosspiece and tied it there. Then he carried it down to the bottom of the long

piece, and so on all around, until he reached the top again. Now the kite frame was finished.

He hurried out to the kitchen to ask Mammy to make him some flour paste. On his way back he stopped at his room for some thin paper he had been saving for months.

He spread the paper out on the floor. He laid the kite frame on top. He weighted it down with some heavy books. With Mother's scissors he cut the paper all around the frame, leaving about a half-inch on all sides. He cut a slit at each place where the edge of the kite turned.

Now came the hard part. Carefully, he pasted the edge of the paper over the string of the frame. With the slits he had cut, he could even turn the corners without a wrinkle.

There! Now, as soon as he made the tail, his kite would be ready to fly.

Mother had been watching him. "Where are you going to fly it?" she asked.

134

"Somewhere outside the city."

"How about Stratford?"

Stratford! Robert jumped up in a hurry. Smith had been doing his arithmetic sums on his slate. When he heard his mother mention the word Stratford, he looked up quickly.

"Not you, Smith," said Mother. "I don't want to take you out of school. They always have a few boarding students at the Academy. We'll let you stay there.

"I can keep on with Robert's lessons, though, wherever we are. Your brother Henry has asked us to come to Stratford for a visit. We'll be there for a week or two. Then we'll go to my family home, Shirley. You can join us there after school is over."

Robert felt sorry for Smith. How he would hate to miss Stratford! But Smith didn't seem too upset. He thought it would be fun to stay at the school.

135

Nat didn't think too much of the idea of taking the kite to Stratford. It was too big. It would be sure to get torn.

"I can mend it," Robert told him.

"It would be easier to make a new one."

"I won't have time. There are too many things to do at Stratford."

At last Nat agreed. He fastened the kite to the back of the carriage. But he was right. It was badly torn when they reached Stratford.

Robert was right, too. He could mend it, and he did.

And Mother certainly had been right also. Stratford was a grand place to fly a kite. Robert went away out in the pasture. There were no trees around, nor any chimneys. All he could see was the blue sky, with white clouds far over his head.

There was a stiff breeze. It caught the kite

136

and flung it up until it almost pulled Robert along, too.

Kite-flying certainly made one hungry. When Robert got back to the house he knew just what a bear felt like. But it was still a long time before the dinner bell would ring.

He opened the gate into the kitchen yard and peeped into the big door of the kitchen. There was no stove there, but the room was hot. All across one side of the wall was a large fireplace.

Big pots of food hung over the fire. They bubbled and steamed. There was an oven, banked with hot coals, where cornbread was baking. A whole row of pies had just come out of the oven. They were still sizzling with rich juice.

In one corner of the kitchen was a wooden block. A young servant was pounding a batch of dough on the block.

"Yum-yum," said Robert. "Beaten biscuit for dinner."

Aunt Cindy was still the cook at Stratford. She turned and saw him. But she wasn't in a good humor today. "Now what do you want in here? I haven't got time to bother with you," she said.

"Please, Aunt Cindy," Robert begged. "I'm

hungry. Can't you give me a little something to tide me over until dinner?"

There was a pan of gingerbread on the table. Aunt Cindy broke off a piece.

"Now you clear out," she said as she gave him the gingerbread.

He went back into the house yard. "I'm thirsty, too," he decided. He started toward the springhouse. There a servant was churning butter. She reached for a gourd dipper and gave him a drink of buttermilk.

"Now," thought Robert, "I reckon I won't starve before dinnertime."

He lay down under the chestnut tree in the yard until he heard a loud bell ring. That meant Aunt Cindy was ready to send the dinner over to the big house.

Robert decided to stay outside and watch. He knew the grown people would eat first, so he didn't need to hurry.

A young servant stood at the top of the outside steps that led to the door nearest the dining room in the big house. Another boy stood halfway down the steps. Two others waited around the kitchen door.

Aunt Cindy brought a large covered platter to the door. She gave it to the nearest child. He carried it proudly across the yard and handed it to the boy on the stairs. He passed it to the boy at the top of the stairs. He, in turn, handed it in to the servant waiting to take it into the dining room.

"It is just like handing buckets down the line at a fire," Robert laughed to himself.

Then he added, out loud, to the boy nearest him, "But I don't see how the food keeps warm."

"Haven't you ever seen a hot water plate?" the boy asked him. He held out the dish of potatoes he was carrying.

Robert looked. The dish had two bottoms,

with a space in between. Aunt Cindy had poured hot water into the space. It would keep the potatoes hot for a long time.

The boy took the dish back and hurried on to the steps.

"I believe," Robert decided, "that I am getting hungry all over again."

He ran inside the house by another door to get ready for dinner.

GRANDFATHER CARTER'S HOME

Robert hated to leave Stratford, but it was good to go to Shirley again, too.

Mother loved Shirley. It was the home where she had been born. She had lived there until she was married.

Shirley was a large house. It was nearly always full of cousins and uncles and aunts. There were plenty of boys for Robert to play with here.

Wild games of scouts and Indians, fishing, swimming—Robert enjoyed them all.

Best of anything, though, were the horses. Again and again, Robert would slip away from the others to go down to the stables.

"When I am a man," he told the stable boys, "I shall have a horse of my own. I had better learn how to take care of one now."

His uncle came into the stable one morning while he was there.

"Would you like to ride out with me?" he asked.

Robert certainly would. "Could I ride the gray mare?" he asked.

"I don't see why not. I've been watching you. You know how to manage a horse right well."

Robert watched his uncle and did just as he did. He made sure the gray mare's blanket was folded exactly right. He sat straight in his saddle, just as his uncle sat.

142

"Ready?" called his uncle.

"All ready."

"Then off we go."

Away they went across the fields. The dogs ran after them. Horseback riding was fun.

GRANDFATHER CARTER

Riding was also hard exercise. Robert was glad to rest later that afternoon. He stretched out on a rug in the hall.

Aunt Randolph was sitting by the fireplace. She was telling the smaller children a story. Robert felt he was growing too big to ask for stories, but he liked to hear them, just the same.

"Your Grandfather Carter was a very rich man," said Aunt Randolph. "He owned miles and miles of land."

"And he had a good many houses, too," said one of the children.

"He did, indeed. And when he went driving, he had six horses to draw his coach."

"Not many boys have a grandfather like that," thought Robert. He watched the Carter grandchildren. They all looked very proud.

"But your Grandfather Carter always said that those who have must share," continued Aunt Randolph.

"Once the corn crop was poor on the James River. Your grandfather brought great wagonloads of corn from some of his other farms. He gave the corn to the neighbors who had none.

"Each year he sent a shipload of tobacco to England to be sold. He would send word that part of the money it brought must be used to help the hungry people of London."

Aunt Randolph paused for a minute and looked at the children. "All of you are Carter grandchildren. Are you going to be like your grandfather?"

"I've always wanted to be just like Father," Robert thought to himself, "but I want to be like Grandfather Carter, too. That certainly is giving myself a lot to live up to."

AN IMPORTANT INVITATION

That night after dinner the children played in the hall. The younger children were playing one game, and the older ones were playing an-

other. The two groups kept getting in each other's way. The older ones scolded. The younger ones were cross.

"Let's all play the same game," said Robert. "Then we won't keep bothering each other."

"Fine! But what game?" Ann asked.

Robert thought quickly. "It must not be too hard for the little children, but it must be fun for the big ones," he said. "Let's play Blindman's Buff."

He tied a handkerchief over the eyes of the oldest girl. Soon he had all the children playing. It was a noisy game, but they were playing together and having a good time.

Aunt Randolph watched Robert. "You like to play with your cousins, don't you?" she asked.

"Yes ma'am," he answered.

"You ought to send him to school at my house," Aunt Randolph told Mother. "Then he could be with his cousins all the time."

"Maybe I shall," replied Mother. "Would you like that, Robert?"

"Indeed I would."

Robert knew about Aunt Randolph's school. Grandfather Carter had twenty-three children. Most of them were married now and had children of their own.

There were so many grandchildren that their parents had started two schools for them. The school for the Carter granddaughters was at Shirley. The school for the Carter grandsons was at Aunt Randolph's.

"It is good that you have such a large house for the boys," said Mother.

"They seem to like it," Aunt Randolph agreed.

"I know I will," said Robert. "I am glad I am a Carter grandson and a nephew of yours."

"Good!" said Aunt Randolph. "And, do you know, some day maybe I'll be proud to be Robert Lee's aunt."

147

Living Up to
Two Names

As soon as the Lees came home from Shirley,
Mother and Ann began to get Robert ready to go
to Aunt Randolph's. They sewed for days and
days.

They made some white shirts with stiff ruffles.
They made a pair of long yellow trousers that
were gathered in at the ankle. The jacket that
went with the trousers was very short and tight.

Robert had never paid very much attention
to his clothes before, but he certainly did like
that jacket.

Mother called him in one afternoon to try on
his new suit.

148

"You look like a man," she said. Then she turned to Ann. "Now, Ann, if I just take this up a little bit here, and let the sleeve down a bit—what do you think?"

"He'll be dressed as fine as any boy in the school," Ann answered.

"It's always a lot of work, though," Robert remembered, "to keep new clothes looking new. I believe I like my old ones better, after all."

He put his old clothes on again and ran off for a last fishing trip with Spec.

"Are the fish going to bite well today?" he asked Spec.

The dog gave a quick yelp.

"Good!" laughed Robert. "I reckon you like fish for supper just as much as I do."

He stopped at a shallow pool to catch some minnows for bait. Then he went on to the river-bank. There he cut himself a pole. He took his line and hook from his pocket and fastened them on. Then he threw his line out over the water. He sat down with his pole and waited for a bite.

Spec caught the scent of a rabbit. He ran off on a hunt of his own.

The day was hot. The sun was bright. Soon Robert decided he would be more comfortable lying down. He threw his free arm over his eyes to keep out the glare of the sunlight.

He was just dozing off to sleep when there came a sharp tug on his line. He sat up with a start. The fishing pole slipped from his hands. Robert made a grab for it, but he was too late. It floated off down the river. He almost fell in, himself.

He felt rather foolish. "I'm glad not even Spec was here to see me lose my pole and line and the fish, too."

Just then Spec came running up. He looked as if he felt rather foolish himself. He hadn't caught his rabbit.

"Don't worry," Robert told him. "Mammy will have some supper for us anyway. And she always says it is more work to fix the fish I bring home than they are worth.

"Come along, Spec. I'll race you across King George's meadows."

They were almost home when Robert saw his Cousin Cassius running toward him.

"Robert," Cassius called. "Come quick!"

"What for?"

Then he heard what for.

Dong! Dong! Dong! came the sound of a great bell.

"Fire!" cried Robert.

"Yes! It's down on Princess Street."

The two boys and Spec ran on. The bell kept ringing.

"Look yonder!" cried Robert. "I can see the smoke."

The street was now full of men and boys. It

looked as if they were running away from the smoke. But Robert knew better.

"They are off to get the fire engine!"

Now they had reached the engine house. They threw open the big doors. They took hold of the long pole at the front of the engine. They pulled the big red engine down the street.

"Stop by the nearest well!" shouted their leader as they came near to the burning house. "Drop the end of the hose down into the well."

The men did as they were told.

"Now! Get ready to man the pump!"

It took twenty men to work the great pump on the engine. There were ten on each side.

"It is like a giant seesaw," Robert said excitedly. "There it goes! Up! Down! Up! Down! But just look how it pumps up the water!"

"You're right!" cried Cassius.

The great pump was drawing the water from the well. It came through the hose with such

force that it reached the upstairs windows of the burning house. The crowd cheered.

Robert didn't know how long he watched, but at last the fire was out. The men rolled up the hose. They began to pull the engine back to the engine house.

Not so many people were anxious to help now. The excitement was over. Robert and Cassius found room on the pole for their own hands. They pulled as hard as they could.

"The fire is out!" they shouted to the women who stood on the sidewalks, looking anxiously down the street.

"But the people who live in the house have nothing left," Robert told Cassius.

"Everything is either burned or soaked with water," Cassius agreed as they started home.

They said good-by at the corner and Robert hurried into the house to tell Mother what had happened.

154

"And the people have nothing at all left," he finished.

He looked around him at the Lees' comfortable furniture and thought of his soft bed upstairs. "Can't we do something about it?" he asked. "I know Grandfather Carter would have helped."

"Of course we aren't as rich as he was," Mother said thoughtfully, "but we ought to be able to do something. Let's go to the storeroom."

They went into the storeroom together and looked over the shelves.

"We can spare a bag of corn meal," said Mother, "and some pickles, if you won't eat quite so many for supper as you have been doing. And there is that bolt of cloth upstairs that I was going to make into sheets. Those poor people will need sheets worse than we do."

"There are my old boots," said Robert thoughtfully. He hated to let those old boots go. There was still a lot of wear left in them.

"Yes," agreed Mother.

It was quite a big-sized bundle that Robert took down to the burned-out home. He talked with the woman of the house for a few moments.

"What do you think she said?" he asked Mother when he came back. "She said, 'Now wasn't it just like your mother to send us these things? She is a Carter through and through.'"

Mother looked pleased. "But it was you who sent the boots," she said.

"Oh, I am a Carter, too. And a Lee. That gives me a double lot to live up to, but I'll have to make a try at it."

AT AUNT RANDOLPH'S SCHOOL

A few days later Robert left for Aunt Randolph's school. All of his clothes were packed in a small leather trunk.

Mother looked sad, and Mildred cried.

156

"Don't you fret," he whispered to her. "Just take care of Mother until I come back."

There was no doubt about it, though. He himself felt sad at first. He had never been away from home without Smith or Mother with him.

Soon, though, the homesickness wore away. He began to enjoy Aunt Randolph's school. He stayed there for nearly a year.

At last he received a letter from his mother.

"Aunt Randolph! Aunt Randolph!" Robert shouted. "Father is on his way home!"

"Wonderful!" said Aunt Randolph. "He has been gone a long time. I doubt that Mildred will even remember him."

"He has been gone since I was a very small boy!" Robert agreed. "Oh, I do hope he is well now."

After that, Robert expected every day to get a letter saying that Father was home. "Then, as soon as he is rested, he'll come here to see me."

But summer turned into early fall and no word came. "Why do you suppose it takes Father so long to get home?" Robert asked his aunt.

"It takes a long time to travel," Aunt Randolph answered. "Besides, he may stop several days here and there to rest."

Still Father did not come. At last Robert learned that Mother had received a letter with bad news in it. Father had died in the spring on his way home. A letter couldn't travel even as fast as a person could, so it had taken several months to arrive.

Not long after the news came, Robert went to Aunt Randolph.

"I believe that I should go home," he said. "Father always told us children that we must take care of Mother."

"And you have," said Aunt Randolph.

"But now Ann is sick," Robert went on. "Mother is sending her up North to see whether she won't get stronger there. Carter is away, going to college."

"What about Smith?"

"He is going into the Navy. He always has wanted to, you know. Now he has a chance to become a midshipman."

"There is still Mildred."

"But she is just a little girl."

"That is true. Maybe your mother does need you."

"Cousin Jim is going down to Alexandria to-morrow. I am going to have him take a letter to Mother. I'll ask her to send for me as soon as she can spare Nat and the carriage."

A few days later Nat arrived.

"How is Mother?" Robert asked first.

The old servant shook his head. "She's poorly. It is hard for her to walk alone."

"She won't have to walk alone," said Robert. "When I get home, I'll help her."

Nat and Robert started home early the next morning. The road led through the woods. The sun shone down on the golden fall leaves. There were brooks and mossy places where the ferns grew thick.

"Tomorrow Smith and I shall go swimming together," Robert told Nat. "Tomorrow will be his last day at home, you know. And we won't get to swim again for a long while."

They drove past large fields of corn. "There were watermelon patches hidden in those cornfields last summer," Robert remembered. "Just thinking about those watermelons makes my mouth water."

"Your mother will have something just as good waiting for your supper," said Nat.

Honeysuckle grew by the side of the road. There were still a few late blossoms. Robert leaned down from the carriage to pick a spray. He held it to his nose.

"Is there anything that smells better than honeysuckle?" he asked.

The old man shook his head. "If there is, I've never smelled it."

He drew the horses to a stop at the top of the hill and pointed with his whip. "Look!"

Robert looked. Far away he could see the steeple of Christ Church and the houses of Alexandria. From that distance they were so small that they looked like dollhouses. Robert tried to imagine which of the houses was his own, but they all looked alike.

"Hurry, Nat!" begged Robert. "I want to get home."

At last the sun went down and twilight fell. Down in the marshy places near the river, the frogs were calling, "Cher-ump! Cher-ump!"

Robert and Nat were silent. They were almost home. The carriage was rattling over the cobblestones of Washington Street. An old man was going slowly down the street. He lighted the oil lamp on the post at each corner.

Nat stopped the horses in front of the small brick house. "Here we are."

Robert jumped from the carriage and ran up the stone steps.

"Mother!" he called. "Mother! I'm home."

In Father's Place

THERE was plenty of work for Robert to do now. His day began in the early morning.

"I'm on my way to market," he told Mammy. "Is there anything special that we need?"

Mammy told him what she had to have in the kitchen.

Then Robert started off whistling. He carried the big market basket over his arm.

The market hadn't changed at all since Robert was a small boy.

"But it seems much smaller," he told the jolly farmer's wife. She still saved a pear or an apple for him every market day.

"It is because you have grown taller," she said. "If you don't stop growing pretty soon, you will have to duck when you go through a door."

Robert laughed. He finished his marketing and hurried home.

"Is Mother awake?" he asked Mammy.

Mammy nodded.

"Then I'll go speak to her while you put breakfast on the table."

Mother was propped up in bed. She looked tired—oh, so very tired. She looked sad, too.

"If I could only make her smile," thought Robert.

He sat down by the side of her bed.

"I heard a good story this morning," he told her. "Everyone at the market was laughing about it. Would you like to hear it?"

Mother smiled faintly. "I always like to hear you tell a story because you enjoy it so much yourself," she said.

164

"Not long ago down in the market in Richmond, there was a young man who had just bought a big turkey," Robert began. "The young man was dressed in fine clothes. He was too proud to be seen carrying a turkey through the streets.

"He saw a countryman in old clothes standing on the corner. He walked over and asked the old man to carry the turkey home for him. 'I will pay you for carrying it,' he said very haughtily.

"The old man took the turkey and followed the young fellow home. Everyone who saw them laughed, but the young man didn't know why.

"The old man carried the turkey to the kitchen door. Then he bowed to the young man and went off down the street.

" 'Who is that old fellow?' the young man asked his neighbor. 'He didn't wait for his money.'

" 'Why, that is John Marshall,' said the neighbor. 'He is the Chief Justice of the United States Supreme Court.' "

Mother laughed out loud. "I know Justice Marshall myself," she said. "It is true that he is one of the most famous men in the United States, but he doesn't look it. He is tall and thin and loves to wear old clothes. And that would be just his idea of a joke." She laughed again.

It was good to see her enjoy his story. Robert felt a little less worried as he went out into the dining room to eat his breakfast.

After breakfast he went back to his room for the house keys. The keys were big and clumsy. Some of them were six inches long. They were too big for his pockets. He had to carry them in a basket.

"I am ready now," he told Mammy when he came back with the keys jingling in his basket. He unlocked the pantry door. Mammy followed him into the pantry.

"It is baking day today, isn't it?" he asked her.
"Then you will need a little of everything."

He gave her flour and eggs and sugar. Then
they went to the storeroom, and then down into
the cellar. At last Mammy had all she would
need for the day.

Now it was almost schooltime. Robert knew
he would have to hurry. He took the key basket
back to his room. He packed up his books.

He was a student at the Academy now. The books that he piled on his slate were Greek and Latin. And his slate wasn't covered with arithmetic any more. It was filled with algebra homework.

Robert carried the slate very carefully. "I don't want to rub off any of the answers I worked so hard over last night," he told himself.

He hurried down the hall for a last look into his mother's room. "Good-by, Mother!"

On his way to school he met several other boys. "What are you doing this afternoon?" they asked. "Let's go fishing down along Hunting Creek."

"I wish I could."

"Why can't you?"

"If the weather is warm and the sun stays out, I have something special to do."

The weather was warm and the sun stayed out. As soon as school was over for the day,

Robert again piled his Greek and Latin books on his slate. Then he hurried home.

"Mother!" he called. "It's such a beautiful day I am going to take you for a drive."

"Not today, Robert. I don't feel like it."

"The doctor said you must get out," Robert answered firmly, "and Mammy has already sent word to Nat to bring the carriage around."

Mother gave in. "Well, if it is a very short ride——"

Mammy hurried to get Mother's shawl and bonnet before she could change her mind. Mrs. Lee hardly ever went out now. It was hard for her to get around.

"Oh, Robert," she said, "I'm afraid that I can't make it to the carriage alone."

"You won't have to," he replied. "Don't you remember what a strong son you have? I'll help you." He took her by the arm and half carried her as she walked to the carriage.

There he piled cushions around her back. "Drive slowly," he told Nat. "We mustn't let her get jolted."

Nat drove very slowly. Mrs. Lee leaned back against the cushions. But Robert was not satisfied. She still looked tired and sad.

"The doctor said these drives wouldn't do her much good unless I found some way to cheer her up," Robert told himself. "I wish I could make her laugh the way she did this morning."

They drove down by the river. There the breeze was cold. Mother shivered a little.

"Goodness," said Robert. "This will never do! How can we keep this wind out?"

There was a newspaper in the carriage. Robert took out the knife he used to mend his pens at school. He cut the newspaper in pieces. Then he pretended to make newspaper curtains to keep out the cold air. He looked so very solemn about his work that Mrs. Lee laughed.

"That's fine!" said Robert. "The drive is really doing you good."

When they got home, tea was ready. Mother ate more than she had for a long time.

"You see," said Robert, "you ought to go out every afternoon. It is good for you."

Mother lay down again after tea. Robert brought his books to her room so that he could be with her while he studied. She watched him as he sat close to the candlelight. His head was bent over his slate.

"Mammy tells me you are working too hard," she said.

Robert shook his head. "Not I!"

"Then why don't you go to bed now?"

"I can't—not until I get this problem right."

He wrote on his slate, then rubbed the answer out and started over. At last he put down his pencil. "There! That is right, and I can prove it."

He stacked his books together. Then he called Mammy to help make Mother comfortable for the night.

Finally he went to his room. In a very short time he was in bed.

Far away he could hear the night watchman. The watchman walked up and down the streets all night. He made sure that everything was safe. He would call out the time of night. He would tell about the weather.

Robert liked to lie in bed and listen to the old

172

man. He could hear him come nearer and nearer down the street.

"Ten o'clock and a clear sky!" called the watchman. Tomorrow would be another good day.

Now the watchman had gone by. His voice sounded farther and farther away.

"Ten o'clock and a clear sky!"

Robert didn't hear him. He was already fast asleep.

Last Days at Home

THE YEAR that Robert was seventeen years old a very famous visitor came to the United States from France. He was the Marquis de Lafayette. When he was a very young man, he had come to America to help the Colonies fight for freedom. Now he was an old man. He wanted to visit the country he had helped to set free.

Thousands of people were waiting at the dock when he reached New York. They cheered and cheered. They had carriages decorated with ribbons. They marched down the street in a big parade.

"Hurrah for Lafayette!" they shouted.

Everywhere he went he was given the same welcome. At last the news came that he would visit Alexandria. Robert was delighted. Lafayette was not only a hero. He had been one of Father's friends, too. Robert wanted very much to see him.

On the day of Lafayette's visit to Alexandria there was no school. The sidewalks were crowded with men, women, and children. They waved flags and cheered.

A big arch had been built across the street down which Lafayette would come. It was decorated with flowers. On the arch was written, "Welcome, Lafayette."

Robert watched the carriage drive through the big arch.

"Hurrah for Lafayette!" he called.

After the parade was over, Robert hurried home to tell Mother about it.

"I saw Lafayette when he came under the

175

arch," he told her. "I had a good look at his face. He is very kind, isn't he?"

"Yes," said Mother. "I have always heard your father say so."

The next morning there was still more excitement in the Lee home. Soon after breakfast a carriage drove up in front of the house. An old man got out.

The Marquis de Lafayette came up the front steps. Nat opened the door for him.

"I should like to see Madame Lee," said Lafayette.

He went in to see Mother. She welcomed him very warmly.

"I heard that the wife of my old friend was still living in Alexandria," Lafayette told Mother. "I wanted to see you."

After they had talked for a few moments, Mother called Robert.

"May I present my son Robert?"

"I am delighted to meet the son of my old friend," said Lafayette.

He told Robert and Mother about his own children. Mostly, though, he talked about Robert's father.

Robert never forgot that morning call. It was a crisp day in October. Nat had built a fire in the fireplace. The burning logs sputtered and sparkled.

In the warm firelight, Robert could see the face of the old gentleman who was Marquis de Lafayette. He could see his mother's face, too. He listened very closely while Mother and Lafayette talked about the brave gentleman who had been his father. Mother's face was aglow with admiration. She could not hide her feelings. "I was very proud of him," she said.

"And some day," said Lafayette, "you are going to be proud of your son, too."

"I am now," said Mother.

It wasn't because of Lafayette's visit that Robert decided to become a soldier. He had been accepted at West Point Military Academy several months before the famous Frenchman called on Mother. But now he felt that he must work harder than ever to get ready.

Mother worked on his clothes. Mammy and Mildred helped her. But Robert was busy, too. He was trying to brush up on his mathematics.

He sat over his slate for hours. With a ruler and pencil he drew his lines very carefully.

"Aren't you almost through?" asked Mother.

"Not quite."

"I put your father's books on your table yesterday. I thought you might like to read again the one he wrote about General Greene."

"I do, as soon as I finish this."

"I thought you told me a while ago that you had the answer."

179

"I have. But now I must copy the problem so that it will be ready to hand in."

After a while there came a whistle under the window.

"Come on, Robert," called Cousin Cassius. "Let's go fishing once more before you leave for West Point."

"Just as soon as I finish this," Robert called back.

His cousin came in to wait. He looked over Robert's shoulder.

"I wouldn't bother about being so careful," he said. "Just as soon as Mr. Hallowell looks at it tomorrow, you'll wash it off."

"But it still ought to look right," said Robert.

He wrote down some more figures. He drew a last line very carefully. Then he looked everything over to make sure there were no mistakes.

"It looks perfect enough to be printed in a book," Cassius teased.

Robert put down his ruler and slate. "It is finished," he said. "Now let's go fishing."

In another week it was time to leave home. Robert's trunk was packed. The horses and carriage were in front of the house. Nat was already in the driver's seat. He was going to drive Robert across the Long Bridge to Washington. Then Robert would travel the rest of the way to West Point by himself.

"We had better be starting," called Nat. "It is getting late."

"I'm coming," said Robert.

"Good-by, Son," said Mother.

He ran down the steps and climbed into the carriage.

The horses started off. Mother watched and waved until Robert was out of sight.

Robert E. Lee—
Soldier and Hero

ROBERT's four years at West Point were busy ones. The boys had to keep their own rooms and scrub their own floors. They had to be up by dawn. They had to study or be in class ten hours a day. From four o'clock until sunset, they drilled.

It wasn't an easy life, but Robert enjoyed it. At last the final examinations began. They weren't just written examinations. The Superintendent of the Academy, the professors, and the board of visitors all sat at two long tables in the front of the room. Five times Robert's name was called. For an hour each time he had to stand before this examining board. He had to answer questions. He had to work problems on the blackboard and explain them. He had to show how much he really knew.

Every member of the class had to go through an examination like this. These examinations lasted for two weeks, but at last they were over. There was nothing to do but wait until the grades were given out.

Then came the afternoon when one of his roommates came running to the barracks. "Robert! Robert! The lists have been posted!"

They hurried to read the lists. Robert had graduated second in the class.

"Into which branch of the army do you want to go?" he was asked. The men with the highest grades were always given first choice.

"I choose the Corps of Engineers," said the new Lieutenant Lee.

"Army engineers always have important work

to do," he told his mother later. "In peacetime, we plan forts. We work to make our rivers deeper and straighter. In wartime we make maps. We build roads and bridges so that the army can get through."

He could also have told her that an army engineer's life was a hard one. Robert was sent to Georgia to build a fort, then to Hampton Roads in Virginia. That was a post he was very glad to get. It wasn't too far from Arlington, where Mary Custis still lived.

At Arlington, in 1831, Robert Edward Lee and Mary Custis were married. Because Mary's father was the adopted son of George Washington, Robert now had another great name to live up to.

For a while Robert and Mary kept house at Hampton Roads. Then Robert was sent out West. The Mississippi River must be straightened. There were dangerous curves that had to be taken out. There were places where a new channel must be cut. It was a tricky piece of work. It called for a good engineer.

That was true, too, of the new fortifications to be built at the New York Harbor. Robert was sent there.

In 1846 this peacetime work stopped suddenly. The War with Mexico broke out. Now, for the first time, Robert saw what war was really like. He heard bullets whistle over his head. He saw dead and dying men around him. He learned what a horrible sight a battlefield could be.

At last the war was over. Robert spent a short while with his family. It was about time. He had been gone so long that he didn't recognize his own little son when the children playing in the yard ran to meet him.

"Where is my boy?" he called. Then he kissed the wrong one!

Now, though, the family could be together again for several years. Robert became Superintendent of West Point Academy. There was a home there for his wife and children.

A soldier never knew, though, where he would be sent next, nor when. In 1855, Robert was sent to Texas to guard the new frontier against the Indians. Colonel Lee was beginning to be a well-known soldier in the United States Army.

THE WAR BETWEEN THE STATES

Robert was also becoming a very worried man. Everywhere he went, people were talking. Some were angry. Some were frightened. All of them were repeating the same word. War! It seemed to be growing closer and closer. Could nothing stop it?

It wouldn't be a war against the Indians. It wouldn't be a war against another country.

Those wars were horrible enough, but this war would be even worse. It would be a war between the states. They had been united since George Washington's day. Now they might be torn apart. Brother might be fighting against brother. There might be times when fathers and sons would be fighting each other.

To which part of the torn country would Robert belong? He hoped he would never have to answer that question. If he did have to, though, he knew that for him there could be only one answer.

He was called back from Texas. That much was good.

"It is surely nice to be with my family, once more," he told his wife.

"I hope you will be here for a long time."

"I hope so, too, but I doubt it."

Down in South Carolina the army of the new Confederate States of America fired on Fort

Sumter. No one was killed on either side, but the War between the States had started.

President Lincoln called for seventy-five thousand volunteers to force the Southern states back into the Union. Who would lead this new army?

Robert received orders to report to Washington. He went promptly, as a soldier must. There he was told, "The President wants to know whether you will take command."

The time had come for Robert to answer the question he had hoped he never would be asked. He shook his head sadly. "I could never fight against the Southern states," he said.

He resigned from the United States Army. Before long, Virginia withdrew from the Union and became one of the Confederate States of America.

Robert was proud of being a Virginian. He wanted to do what he could to help the state that

he loved so much. He became head of Virginia's army. Later, he became the Commanding General of the whole Confederate Army.

The war was long and hard. The years went slowly. At last, in 1865, General Lee knew that his soldiers could not fight any longer. They had no supplies. They had no food. There was but one thing for him to do.

He asked for a meeting with General Grant, the Commanding General of the Union Army. The two generals met at Appomattox Courthouse, Virginia, and arranged for the surrender of the Confederate Army.

AFTER THE WAR

Throughout the South everyone loved and admired General Robert E. Lee. His soldiers and their families looked to him for leadership. What should they do next?

"The war is over," he told them. "We must learn to live in peace with our neighbors. There is no room for hate."

He set them a good example.

But how should he make a living for himself? Like many other Southerners, he had lost his home and all that he owned in the war. His days as a soldier were over.

"Come with us," a group of businessmen told him. "We will pay you a good salary. You won't have any work to do. We just want your name. People all over the South will be sure that our business is a good one if you are with us. They will put money in our company."

General Lee said "No." He had very little left now except his fine name. He would still take good care of that.

Washington College, in Virginia, asked him to be its president. He thought about this offer. "It will be good to train young men," he decided. "I shall be proud to have my name connected with a good college."

He gave the rest of his life to this work. His name stayed with the school. After his death, Washington College became Washington and Lee University.

It was not only at the University that he was remembered. All over the country—North, South, East and West—people loved and honored the great hero of the South: General Robert E. Lee, of Virginia.